LITTLE LEARNER PACKETS

PHONICS

Violet Findley

Cover design: Tannaz Fassihi; Cover art: Jason Dove
Interior design: Michelle H. Kim
Interior illustrator: Doug Jones

ISBN: 978-1-338-22828-1
Copyright © 2018 by Scholastic Inc.
All rights reserved.
Printed in the U.S.A.
First printing, January 2018.

1 2 3 4 5 6 7 8 9 10   40   23 22 21 20 19 18

Table of Contents

Introduction

Looking for a playful way to help children master short and long vowel sounds? Welcome to *Little Learner Packets: Phonics*! The 10 reproducible learning packets in this book provide targeted practice to hardwire phonological awareness and set the stage for decoding success.

Each packet invites children to read, trace, write, graph, match, find, unscramble, and gain lots of experience with the target vowel sound. You can use the learning packets in a variety of ways and with children of all learning styles. Children can complete the activities at their seats or in a learning center. Or they can use the pages as take-home practice.

The packets are ideal for encouraging children to work independently and at their own pace. A grid on the introduction page of each packet lets children track their progress as they complete each page. Best of all, the activities support children in meeting the standards for Reading Foundational Skills for Kindergarten and First Grade. (See the Connections to the Standards box.)

Connections to the Standards

Print Concepts
Demonstrate understanding of the organization and basic features of print.

Phonological Awareness
Demonstrate understanding of spoken words, syllables, and sounds.

Phonics and Word Recognition
Know and apply grade-level phonics and word analysis skills in decoding words.

Phonics Packets

PACKET 1: short *a*

PACKET 2: short *e*

PACKET 3: short *i*

PACKET 4: short *o*

PACKET 5: short *u*

PACKET 6: long *a*

PACKET 7: long *e*

PACKET 8: long *i*

PACKET 9: long *o*

PACKET 10: long *u*

How to Use the Phonics Packets

Copy a class supply of the eight pages for the phonics packet you want to use. Then sequence and staple each set of pages together and distribute the packets to children. All they need to complete the pages are pencils and crayons. TIP: To conserve paper, simply make double-sided copies.

The format of the learning packets makes them very easy to use. Here's what you'll find on each page:

Page 1 / Introduction: This page introduces the packet's target vowel sound, such as short *a*. Children trace the words on the page. When the activity is finished, children color in the first box in the tracking grid at the bottom. As they complete each of the remaining pages in the packet, children will color in the corresponding box in this grid.

Pages 2 & 3 / Read & Write: Children read the illustrated "story sentence" featuring words with the target sound. They then write those words several times to boost phonological awareness and handwriting skills.

Page 4 / Color: At the top of the page, children build decoding and discrimination skills by using a crayon to color boxes that contain words with the target vowel sound. At the bottom of the page, children build math skills by counting the number of boxes they colored.

Page 5 / Graph: The fun graphing activity gives children the opportunity to reinforce phonics skills and counting skills simultaneously. TIP: Extend math learning by inviting children to explore and discuss the graph's results.

Page 6 / Match & Find: At the top of the page, children reinforce discrimination skills by identifying words with the target vowel sound. At the bottom of the page, children locate each word in a simple hidden-word puzzle. NOTE: Each sight word appears in the puzzle once, horizontally.

Page 7 / Unscramble: This page provides additional phonics practice by challenging children to unscramble words with the target vowel sound. As they do, children will develop fine-motor skills, too!

Page 8 / Review: Children complete a humorous, illustrated story by writing words with the target sound in the appropriate blanks. TIP: When the blanks are filled in, boost early literacy skills by running your finger under the text and reading the story aloud together.

Answer Key: A handy answer key is provided on pages 87–96. The thumbnail images allow you to check children's completed pages at a glance. You can then use the results to determine areas in which they might need additional instruction or practice.

Teaching Tips

Use these tips to help children get the most from the learning packets.

* **Provide a model:** Demonstrate, step by step, how to complete each page in the first packet. Children should then be able to complete the remaining packets independently.

* **Focus on the target-sound words:** Have children identify each word with the target sound and write it in the air. You can also work together to brainstorm a list of other words that contain that target vowel sound.

* **Offer additional practice:** Play phonics games. Listen to phonics songs. Write phonics stories. And, of course, read, read, read!

Learning Centers

You might label a separate folder with each child's name and place the packets in the folder to keep in a learning center. Then children can retrieve the assigned packet and work independently through the pages during center time. To make the packets self-checking, you can enlarge the answer keys for each packet, cut apart the images, then sequence and staple them together to create a mini answer key for that packet. Finally, place all of the answer keys in the center. Children can refer to the answer key that corresponds to the packet they are working on to check their completed pages.

Ways to Use the Phonics Learning Packets

Children can work through the packets at their own pace, tracking their progress as they complete each page. The packets are ideal for the following:

* Learning center activity
* Independent seatwork
* One-on-one lesson

* Morning starter
* End of the day wrap-up
* Take-home practice

Let's learn phonics!

Assessing Learning

To quickly assess children's phonics skills, do the following:

* Display words with each target sound and have children read them aloud.

* Call out words with each target sound and have children write them down.

* Call out a target sound and have children respond with words containing that sound.

Name: _____

PHONICS
short *a*

Hi!

bat
cap
van
mad

Trace each word above. Color in each box when you complete the activity.

① Introduction	② Read & Write	③ Read & Write	④ Color
⑤ Graph	⑥ Match & Find	⑦ Unscramble	⑧ Review

Name: _____

Read the sentence.

The <u>bat</u> is <u>glad</u> he <u>has</u> a <u>cap</u>.

Trace and write the short-*a* words.

bat

glad

has

cap

8

Name: _____

Read the sentence.

The bat is <u>**mad**</u> <u>**at**</u> <u>**that**</u> <u>**cat**</u>!

Trace and write the short-*a* words.

mad

at

that

cat

9

Name: _____

Find the short-*a* words. Color them  **yellow** .

bat

fan

tack

bed

sock

lamp

bag

duck

cat

fish

cab

cap

How many blocks have short-*a* words? Circle the number.

1   2   3   4   5   6   7   8   9   10

Little Learner Packets: Phonics © Scholastic Inc.

Name: _____

Count and graph the short-*a* words.

mat   cab   van

bat

van   bat

mat   van   bat

bat

bat	**van**	**cab**	**mat**

4

3

2

1

Draw lines to match the bat with the short-*a* words.

 ant •

 fish •

 cat •

 lamp •

 egg •

• pants

• doll

• fan

• bug

• pin

Find and circle each short-*a* word once.

Word Bank	
ant	e x l a m p b r
fan	a n t q v u x r
cat	v b o m f a n h
lamp	p l n c a t z c
pants	m r p a n t s d

Name: _____

Unscramble each short-*a* word.

Word Bank

| lamp | van | cat | bag |
| mask | bat | man | ant |

atb
_____

nav
_____

tac
_____

sakm
_____

pmal
_____

abg
_____

nam
_____

nat
_____

FOR YOU!

Fill in each short-*a* word once to complete the story. Then read it aloud.

Word Bank	cat	sat	glad	ant	bat	cap

The New Cap

GOOD JOB!

The bat _____ on a mat.

Along came a furry _____.

The cat had a new _____.

It had an _____ on it!

The cap was for the _____.

That made the bat _____!

Little Learner Packets: Phonics © Scholastic Inc.

Name: _____

PHONICS
short e

Hi!

hen

bell

nest

elf

Trace each word above. Color in each box when you complete the activity.

① Introduction	② Read & Write	③ Read & Write	④ Color
⑤ Graph	⑥ Match & Find	⑦ Unscramble	⑧ Review

PHONICS 2
Introduction
1

Read the sentence.

FOR YOU!

An <u>elf</u> in a <u>vest</u> gave the <u>hen</u> a <u>chest</u>.

Trace and write the short-e words.

elf

vest

hen

chest

Name: _____

Read the sentence.

A <u>shell</u>, <u>pen</u>, <u>bell</u>, and <u>dress</u> were in the chest.

Trace and write the short-*e* words.

shell

pen

bell

dress

Name: _____

Find the short-*e* words. Color them  blue .

How many blocks have short-*e* words? Circle the number.

1 2 3 4 5 6 7 8 9 10

Name: _____

PHONICS 2
Graph
5

Count and graph the short-*e* words.

hen

shell

shell

web

shell

nest

shell

hen

hen

web

hen	web	shell	nest

4

3

2

1

Little Learner Packets: Phonics © Scholastic Inc.

19

Name: _____

Draw lines to match the hen with the short-*e* words.

 clock •

 bed •

 egg •

 bug •

 tent •

• cap

• fox

• vest

• pen

• pig

Find and circle each short-*e* word once.

Word Bank								
vest	y	c	t	e	n	t	a	d
bed	b	e	d	t	z	u	m	n
egg	q	k	o	p	f	p	e	n
pen	r	a	s	e	g	g	n	h
tent	u	g	c	v	e	s	t	i

Name: _____

Unscramble each short-e word.

Word Bank	hen	elf	egg	leg
	tent	web	vest	nest

svet

_____

geg

_____

snet

_____

bew

_____

nett

_____

fle

_____

neh

_____

gle

_____

Fill in each short-e word once to complete the story. Then read it aloud.

Word Bank	hen elf pen then dress end

The Best Chest

The red _____ got the best chest!

It was from the _____.

A dress and _____ were in it.

The hen wore the _____

and _____ she wrote a note

with the pen. The _____.

Name: _____

PHONICS
short i

Hi!

pig ~~pig~~

bib ~~bib~~

fish ~~fish~~

ring ~~ring~~

Trace each word above. Color in each box when you complete the activity.

①	②	③	④
Introduction	**Read & Write**	**Read & Write**	**Color**
⑤	⑥	⑦	⑧
Graph	**Match & Find**	**Unscramble**	**Review**

Name: _____

Read the sentence.

The **pig** **is** in a very **big** **wig**.

Trace and write the short-*i* words.

pig

is

big

wig

Name: _____

Read the sentence.

The pig **in** the wig wears a **bib** to **lick** **six** lollipops.

Trace and write the short-*i* words.

in

bib

lick

six

Name: _____

Find the short-*i* words. Color them pink.

dig

pig

fish

hen

bug

chick

dog

pin

six

rug

wig

bed

How many blocks have short-*i* words? Circle the number.

1   2   3   4   5   6   7   8   9   10

Name: _____

Count and graph the short-*i* words.

pig

ring   fish   six

fish   pig   ring

ring   ring   pig

pig	fish	ring	six
4			
3			
2			
1			

Name: _____

Draw lines to match the pig with the short-*i* words.

 ring •

 rug •

 dig •

 mop •

 fish •

• bat

• pin

• kid

• clock

• bag

Find and circle each short-*i* word once.

Word Bank	
ring	e c f i s h k d
kid	t d i g t y o b
dig	d y u x p i n j
fish	k i d n q e d v
pin	b a r i n g m z

28

Little Learner Packets: Phonics · Phonics © Scholastic Inc.

Name: _____

Unscramble each short-*i* word.

Word Bank	pig	kid	wig	pin
	ring	six	fish	bib

gip
_____

shif
_____

wgi
_____

nirg
_____

ixs
_____

ibb
_____

idk
_____

pni
_____

Name: _____

OINK!

Fill in each short-*i* word once to complete the story. Then read it aloud.

Word Bank	pig in fish Splish kid wig

The Pig in a Wig

"Oink!" said the _____.

She was _____ a boat

with a nice _____.

_____, splash!

A _____ jumped up!

The fish has a big _____, too!

GOOD JOB!

30

Little Learner Packets: Phonics © Scholastic Inc.

Name: _____

PHONICS
short o

dog   dog

fox   fox

rock   rock

mop   mop

Trace each word above. Color in each box when you complete the activity.

① Introduction	② Read & Write	③ Read & Write	④ Color
⑤ Graph	⑥ Match & Find	⑦ Unscramble	⑧ Review

Name: _____

Read the sentence.

The **<u>dog</u>** and **<u>frog</u>** sit **<u>on</u>** a **<u>log</u>**.

Trace and write the short-*o* words.

dog

frog

on

log

Name: _____

Read the sentence.

A <u>fox</u> gave them a <u>box</u> with <u>lots</u> of <u>clocks</u>.

Trace and write the short-*o* words.

fox

box

lots

clocks

Name: _____

Find the short-*o* words. Color them green .

sock

frog

fish

dog

cat

log

doll

tub

bed

mop

egg

fox

How many blocks have short-*o* words? Circle the number.

1 2 3 4 5 6 7 8 9 10

34

Name: _____

Count and graph the short-*o* words.

 dog	 fox	 rock	 stop
4			
3			
2			
1			

Name: _____

Draw lines to match the dog with the short-*o* words.

 bell •

 clock •

 pig •

 bag •

 mop •

• log

• cup

• duck

• frog

• box

Find and circle each short-*o* word once.

Word Bank							
frog	c	g	a	b	o	x	k	d
mop	q	t	c	l	o	c	k	n
clock	w	e	r	x	m	o	p	u
log	l	o	g	m	s	e	t	v
box	u	r	f	r	o	g	z	f

Little Learner Packets: Phonics © Scholastic Inc.

Name: _____

Unscramble each short-*o* word.

Word Bank	fox	frog	ox	doll
	mop	rock	pot	sock

kcos _____

fxo _____

cokr _____

xo _____

pmo _____

llod _____

opt _____

grof _____

FOR YOU!

Fill in each short-*o* word once to complete the story. Then read it aloud.

Word Bank	lots	tock	doll	dog	sock	of

The Box of Clocks

GOOD JOB!

Fox gave _____ and frog a box.

The box had _____ of clocks!

Some _____ the clocks were silly.

One clock looked like a pretty _____!

One clock looked like a stinky _____!

Tick, _____!

Little Learner Packets: Phonics © Scholastic Inc.

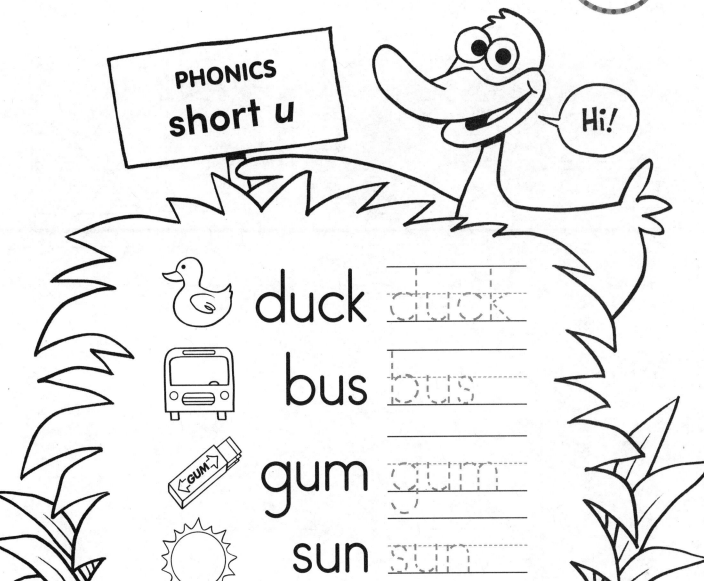

Trace each word above. Color in each box when you complete the activity.

① Introduction	② Read & Write	③ Read & Write	④ Color
⑤ Graph	⑥ Match & Find	⑦ Unscramble	⑧ Review

Name: _____

Read the sentence.

A <u>duck</u> in a <u>truck</u> saw his pals <u>run</u>
to get the <u>bus</u>.

Trace and write the short-*u* words.

duck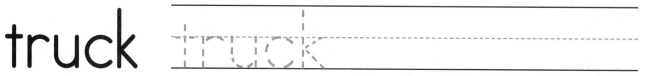

truck

run

bus

Name: _____

Read the sentence.

The duck told the **pup** and **skunk** to **just** **jump** in his truck.

Trace and write the short-*u* words.

pup

skunk

just

jump

Name: _____

PHONICS 5
Color
4

Find the short-*u* words. Color them orange.

duck bug

jug bag

rock bus web mug

rug pig skunk pup

How many blocks have short-*u* words? Circle the number.

1 2 3 4 5 6 7 8 9 10

42

Little Learner Packets: Phonics © Scholastic Inc.

Name: _____

Count and graph the short-*u* words.

	duck	sun	bus	gum
4				
3				
2				
1				

Name: _____

Draw lines to match the duck with the short-*u* words.

 skunk •

 cab •

 drum •

hen •

 rug •

• gum

• nest

• pup

• box

• wig

Find and circle each short-*u* word once.

Word Bank	
skunk	c x a r u g j e
pup	t o s k u n k m
drum	h j e l p u p t
gum	d r u m z i n v
rug	c a d g u m t i

Little Learner Packets: Phonics © Scholastic Inc.

Name: _____

Unscramble each short-*u* word.

Word Bank	duck	jug	bug	pup
	drum	bus	cup	truck

gub _____

uckd _____

ujg _____

usb _____

rumd _____

puc _____

upp _____

kcutr _____

Name: _____

Fill in each short-*u* word once to complete the story. Then read it aloud.

Word Bank	up	fun	duck	cups	yum	sun

Up the Hill

The _____, pup, and skunk

went _____ a big hill.

Then they sat in the warm _____

and drank _____ of tea.

Yum, _____!

It was so _____!

GOOD JOB!

Name: _____

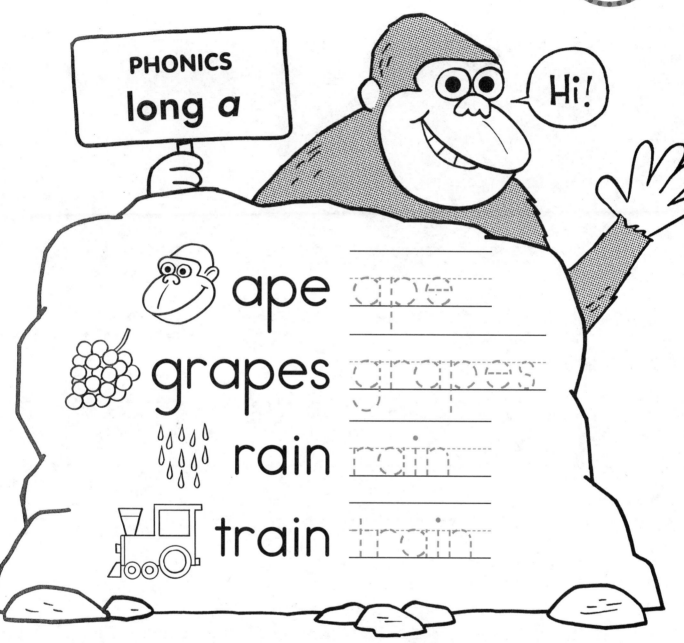

PHONICS
long *a*

Hi!

ape   ape

grapes   grapes

rain   rain

train   train

Trace each word above. Color in each box when you complete the activity.

1 Introduction	2 Read & Write	3 Read & Write	4 Color
5 Graph	6 Match & Find	7 Unscramble	8 Review

Name: _____

Read the sentence.

The <u>ape</u> on <u>skates</u> eats <u>cake</u> and <u>grapes</u>.

Trace and write the long-*a* words.

ape

skates

cake

grapes

48

Read the sentence.

The ape plays with his <u>train</u>, <u>snail</u>, and <u>pail</u> in the <u>rain</u>.

Trace and write the long-*a* words.

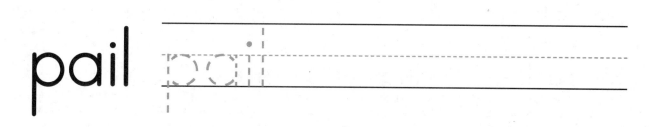

train

snail

pail

rain

Name: _____

Find the long-*a* words. Color them 🖍 (red) .

How many blocks have long-*a* words? Circle the number.

1   2   3   4   5   6   7   8   9   10

Name: _____

Count and graph the long-*a* words.

ape	plane	train	paint
4			
3			
2			
1			

Name: _____

Draw lines to match the ape with the long-*a* words.

 kite •

 cake •

 mule •

 feet •

 train •

• bike

• wave

• gate

• rope

• snake

Find and circle each long-*a* word once.

Word Bank								
snake	t	r	a	i	n	p	b	r
cake	a	n	t	q	c	a	k	e
gate	v	g	a	t	e	a	n	d
wave	p	l	s	n	a	k	e	c
train	m	r	p	w	a	v	e	x

Little Learner Packets: Phonics © Scholastic Inc.

Name: _____

Unscramble each long-*a* word.

Word Bank

pail	snake	wave	cake
rain	snail	ape	nail

pae _____

ekac _____

vwae _____

anir _____

lasin _____

naske _____

liap _____

ilan _____

Name: _____

Fill in each long-_a_ word once to complete the story. Then read it aloud.

Word Bank	ape whale gave paint made snail

Ape's Painting

The _____ is an artist.

He loves to _____.

He _____ a picture

of a _____ in the rain.

He _____ it to the snail.

"I love it!" said the _____.

54

Little Learner Packets: Phonics © Scholastic Inc.

Name: _____

PHONICS
long e

Hi!

seal
leaf
bee
tree

Trace each word above. Color in each box when you complete the activity.

① Introduction	② Read & Write	③ Read & Write	④ Color
⑤ Graph	⑥ Match & Find	⑦ Unscramble	⑧ Review

Read the sentence.

The **seal** likes to **eat** ice **cream** on the **beach**.

Trace and write the long-*e* words.

seal

eat

cream

beach

Name: _____

Read the sentence.

The seal goes to **sleep** and dreams about **three** **bees** and **cheese**.

Trace and write the long-*e* words.

sleep

three

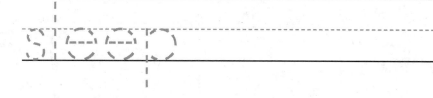

bees

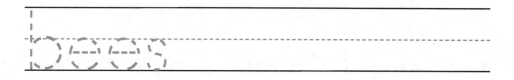

cheese

Little Learner Packets: Phonics © Scholastic Inc.

57

Name: _____

Find the long-*e* words. Color them [crayon] purple .

seal

tree

beach   mice

queen   skate   feet   leaf

bee   boat   jeans   cube

How many blocks have long-*e* words? Circle the number.

1   2   3   4   5   6   7   8   9   10

Little Learner Packets: Phonics © Scholastic Inc.

Name: _____

Count and graph the long-*e* words.

	 seal	jeep	cheese	teeth
4				
3				
2				
1				

Little Learner Packets: Phonics © Scholastic Inc.

Name: _____

Draw lines to match the seal with the long-*e* words.

 queen •

 grapes •

 feet •

 bike •

 cube •

• peach

• jeans

• skate

• phone

• tree

Find and circle each long-*e* word once.

Word Bank	
queen jeans peach feet tree	i y p e a c h o x t r e e s u k v h f e e t n d w o g j e a n s q u e e n p x z

60

Little Learner Packets: Phonics © Scholastic Inc.

Name: _____

Unscramble each long-e word.

Word Bank	bee jeep leaf feet
	cheese seal wheel sheep

lase

_____

efet

_____

fael

_____

eeechs

_____

ebe

_____

eehwl

_____

epje

_____

heeps

_____

Name: _____

BEEP! BEEP!

Fill in each long-*e* word once to complete the story. Then read it aloud.

Word Bank	beach	queen	jeep
	sea	beep	sheep

Seal at the Beach

Seal is at a sandy _____.

He sees a _____

standing in the _____.

He sees a queen driving

in a _____.

The _____ toots her horn.

Beep, _____!

GOOD JOB!

Little Learner Packets: Phonics © Scholastic Inc.

Name: _____

PHONICS
long *i*

Hi!

mice ~~mice~~

kite ~~kite~~

ice ~~ice~~

five ~~five~~

Trace each word above. Color in each box when you complete the activity.

① Introduction	② Read & Write	③ Read & Write	④ Color
⑤ Graph	⑥ Match & Find	⑦ Unscramble	⑧ Review

63

Name: _____

Read the sentence.

The **mice ride** a **bike** as the sun **shines**.

Trace and write the long-*i* words.

mice

ride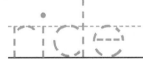

bike

shines

Read the sentence.

The **nice** mice fly **five** **kites** near a **slide**.

Trace and write the long-*i* words.

nice

five

kites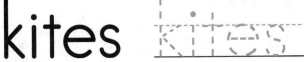

slide

Name: _____

Find the long-*i* words. Color them  brown .

How many blocks have long-*i* words? Circle the number.

1   2   3   4   5   6   7   8   9   10

Little Learner Packets: Phonics © Scholastic Inc.

Name: _____

Count and graph the long-*i* words.

nine

mice   mice

kite

nine   nine

dime

nine

mice   dime

mice	kite	nine	dime
4			
3			
2			
1			

Name: _____

Draw lines to match the mice with the long-*i* words.

 queen •

 hive •

 jeep •

9 nine •

 mule •

• bike

• kite

• plate

• coat

• five 5

Find and circle each long-*i* word once.

Word Bank	
bike hive nine kite five	h i v e m p b r a n i n e u x r v b o m k i t e p b i k e t z c m r f i v e s d

Name: _____

Unscramble each long-*i* word.

Word Bank

mice	rice	tire	kite
ice	fire	nine	hive

cime _____

evih _____

cie _____

riet _____

erif _____

teki _____

nnei _____

ceir _____

Name: _____

Fill in each long-*i* word once to complete the story. Then read it aloud.

Word Bank	like dive slide cried mice nice

The Nice Pool Party

GOOD JOB!

"What a _____ day for

a pool party!" said the _____.

One mouse did a fine _____.

One mouse slid down a _____.

"We really _____ playing

in the water!" they _____.

70

Name: _____

PHONICS
long o

Hi!

goat goat

boat boat

nose nose

rope rope

Trace each word above. Color in each box when you complete the activity.

① Introduction	② Read & Write	③ Read & Write	④ Color
⑤ Graph	⑥ Match & Find	⑦ Unscramble	⑧ Review

Little Learner Packets: Phonics © Scholastic Inc.

71

Read the sentence.

The **goat** wears a **coat** when he **floats** in a **boat**.

Trace and write the long-*o* words.

goat

coat

floats

boat

Name: _____

Read the sentence.

The goat sees an **old toad** with a **rose** in a **slow** boat.

Trace and write the long-*o* words.

old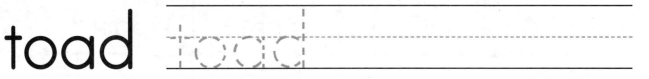

toad

rose

slow

Name: _____

Find the long-*o* words. Color them  grey .

goat

coat   boat   globe

road   queen   cake   toast

cone   plate   rose   kite

How many blocks have long-*o* words? Circle the number.

1   2   3   4   5   6   7   8   9   10

Name: _____

Count and graph the long-*o* words.

goat   rose

soap   soap

          rose

smoke   soap

goat   goat   soap

	goat	soap	rose	smoke
4				
3				
2				
1				

Name: _____

Draw lines to match the goat with the long-*o* words.

 soap •

 bike •

 phone •

jeep •

rope •

• cube

• boat

• nose

• rain

• snail

Find and circle each long-*o* word once.

Word Bank							
boat	r o p e k e q z
soap	a b h s o a p w
phone	g p h o n e i d
nose	n o s e m y u t
rope	t g a b o a t c

Name: _____

PHONICS 9
Unscramble
7

Unscramble each long-*o* word.

Word Bank	nose soap rope road boat goat phone hole

taog

_____

posa

_____

atob

_____

poer

_____

seno

_____

adro

_____

leho

_____

enoph

_____

Little Learner Packets: Phonics © Scholastic Inc.

77

Name: _____

Fill in each long-*o* word once to complete the story. Then read it aloud.

Word Bank	phone goat joke toad so boat

The Goat in a Boat

The goat in a _____

uses his cell _____

to call the old _____.

Then the _____

tells the old toad a _____.

The joke is _____ funny!

Little Learner Packets: Phonics © Scholastic Inc.

Name: _____

PHONICS
long *u*

Hi!

mule
cube
flute
human

Trace each word above. Color in each box when you complete the activity.

① Introduction	② Read & Write	③ Read & Write	④ Color
⑤ Graph	⑥ Match & Find	⑦ Unscramble	⑧ Review

Name: _____

Read the sentence.

The <u>cute</u> <u>mule</u> stood on a <u>huge</u> <u>cube</u>.

Trace and write the long-*u* words.

cute

mule

huge

cube

Little Learner Packets: Phonics © Scholastic Inc.

Read the sentence.

The mule **used** a **flute** to play **music** for a **unicorn**.

Trace and write the long-*u* words.

used

flute

music

unicorn

Name: _____

Find the long-*u* words. Color them  (blue) **.**

mule

dune

flute

cube

bee

music

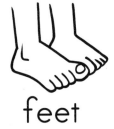

feet

boat

cave

tube

ape

unicorn

How many blocks have long-*u* words? Circle the number.

1   2   3   4   5   6   7   8   9   10

Little Learner Packets: Phonics © Scholastic Inc.

Name: _____

Count and graph the long-*u* words.

cube   mule

dune

tube   tube   cube

mule

tube   cube   tube

mule	cube	tube	dune

4

3

2

1

Name: _____

Draw lines to match the mule with the long-*u* words.

 pin •

 tube •

 fish •

 bug •

 human •

 • dune

• doll

• cube

• egg

• music

Find and circle each long-*u* word once.

Word Bank	
cube	d u n e s i m x
tube	d h c u b e q r
dune	k h u m a n o t
music	t u b e n y a r
human	h y m u s i c d

84

Name: _____

Unscramble each long-*u* word.

Word Bank

mule	bugle	dune	cube
flute	music	tube	unicorn

elum _____

beut _____

ebcu _____

etulf _____

simcu _____

nedu _____

corninu _____

glueb _____

Fill in each long-*u* word once to complete the story. Then read it aloud.

Word Bank	bugle mule huge flute unicorn cube

The Mule and the Unicorn

The _____ has spots!

The _____ has stars!

They sit on a _____.

It is so _____!

The mule plays a _____.

The unicorn plays a _____.

They make beautiful music!

GOOD JOB!

Answer Key

PACKET 1

PHONICS

short *a*

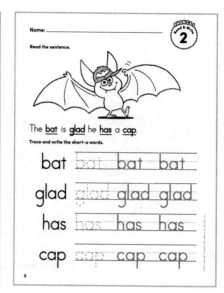

Name: _____

PHONICS Introduction 1

PHONICS
short *a*

Hi!

bat **bat**
cap **cap**
van **van**
mad **mad**

Trace each word above. Color in each box when you complete the activity.

| 1 Introduction | 2 Read & Write | 3 Read & Write | 4 Color |
| 5 Graph | 6 Match & Find | 7 Unscramble | 8 Review |

7

Name: _____

PHONICS Read & Write 2

Read the sentence.

The <u>bat</u> is <u>glad</u> he <u>has</u> a <u>cap</u>.

Trace and write the short-*a* words.

bat **bat bat bat**
glad **glad glad glad**
has **has has has**
cap **cap cap cap**

8

Name: _____

PHONICS Read & Write 3

Read the sentence.

The bat is <u>mad at that cat</u>!

Trace and write the short-*a* words.

mad **mad mad mad**
at **at at at**
that **that that that**
cat **cat cat cat**

9

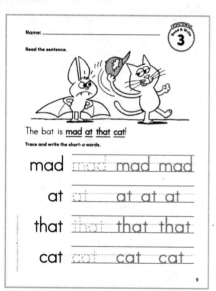

Name: _____

PHONICS Color 4

Find the short-*a* words. Color them yellow.

bat · fan
tack · bed
sock · lamp · bag · duck
cat · fish · cab · cap

How many blocks have short-*a* words? Circle the number.

1 2 3 4 5 6 7 (8) 9 10

10

Name: _____

PHONICS Graph 5

Count and graph the short-*a* words.

mat cab bat van
mat van van bat
bat van bat

	bat	van	cab	mat
4				
3				
2				
1				

11

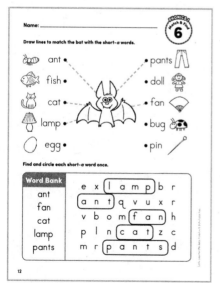

Name: _____

PHONICS Match & Find 6

Draw lines to match the bat with the short-*a* words.

ant • • pants
fish • • doll
cat • • fan
lamp • • bug
egg • • pin

Find and circle each short-*a* word once.

Word Bank
ant
fan
cat
lamp
pants

e x l a m p b r
a n t q v u x r
v b o m f a n h
p l n c a t z c
m r p a n t s d

12

Name: _____

PHONICS Unscramble 7

Unscramble each short-*a* word.

Word Bank | lamp van cat bag | mask bat man ant

atb **bat**
nav **van**
tac **cat**
sakm **mask**
pmal **lamp**
abg **bag**
nam **man**
nat **ant**

13

Name: _____

PHONICS Review 8

FOR YOU!

Fill in each short-*a* word once to complete the story. Then read it aloud.

Word Bank cat sat glad ant bat cap

The New Cap

The bat __sat__ on a mat.
Along came a furry __cat__
The cat had a new __cap__
It had an __ant__ on it!
The cap was for the __bat__
That made the bat __glad__ |

GOOD JOB!

14

87

PACKET 2

PHONICS

short *e*

PHONICS
short *e*

Hi!

hen hen
bell bell
nest nest
elf elf

Trace each word above. Color in each box when you complete the activity.

| 1 Introduction | 2 Read & Write | 3 Read & Write | 4 Color |
| 5 Graph | 6 Match & Find | 7 Unscramble | 8 Review |

15

Name: _____

Read the sentence.

FOR YOU!

An <u>elf</u> in a <u>vest</u> gave the <u>hen</u> a <u>chest</u>.

Trace and write the short-*e* words.

elf   elf elf elf elf
vest   vest vest vest
hen   hen hen hen
chest chest chest

16

Name: _____

Read the sentence.

A <u>shell</u>, <u>pen</u>, <u>bell</u>, and <u>dress</u> were in the chest.

Trace and write the short-*e* words.

shell shell shell shell
pen   pen pen pen
bell   bell bell bell
dress dress dress

17

Name: _____

Find the short-*e* words. Color them ☐ blue .

hen   egg
nest   cat
dog vest shell tent
mug bag ten pig

How many blocks have short-*e* words? Circle the number.

1 2 3 4 5 6 (7) 8 9 10

18

Name: _____

Count and graph the short-*e* words.

hen shell shell
shell web nest
web hen shell hen

	🐔 hen	🕸 web	🐚 shell	🪹 nest
4				
3				
2				
1				

19

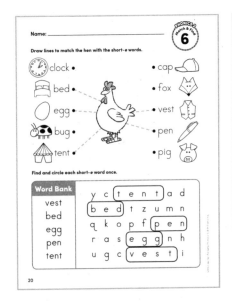

Name: _____

Draw lines to match the hen with the short-*e* words.

🕐 clock •   • cap 🧢
🛏 bed •   • fox 🦊
🥚 egg •   • vest 🦺
🐞 bug •   • pen 🖊
⛺ tent •   • pig 🐷

Find and circle each short-*e* word once.

Word Bank
vest
bed
egg
pen
tent

y c t e n t a d
b e d t z u m n
q k o p f p e n
r a s e g g n h
u g c v e s t i

20

Name: _____

Unscramble each short-*e* word.

Word Bank hen elf egg leg
tent web vest nest

svet → vest
geg → egg
snet → nest
bew → web
nett → tent
fle → elf
neh → hen
gle → leg

21

Name: _____

FOR YOU!

DEAR ELF THANKS FOR THE CHEST. LOVE, HEN

Fill in each short-*e* word once to complete the story. Then read it aloud.

Word Bank hen elf pen then dress end

The Best Chest

The red __hen__ got the best chest!
It was from the __elf__
A dress and __pen__ were in it.
The hen wore the __dress__
and __then__ she wrote a note
with the pen. The __end__

GOOD JOB!

22

88

Little Learner Packets: Phonics © Scholastic Inc.

PACKET 3

PHONICS

short *i*

PHONICS i
Introduction
1

pig pig
bib bib
fish fish
ring ring

Trace each word above. Color in each box when you complete the activity.

| ① Introduction | ② Read & Write | ③ Read & Write | ④ Color |
| ⑤ Graph | ⑥ Match & Find | ⑦ Unscramble | ⑧ Review |

23

Name: _____

PHONICS i
Read & Write
2

Read the sentence.

The **pig is** in a very **big wig**.

Trace and write the short-*i* words.

pig pig pig pig

is is is is

big big big big

wig wig wig wig

24

Name: _____

PHONICS i
Read & Write
3

Read the sentence.

The pig **in** the wig wears a **bib** to **lick** **six** lollipops.

Trace and write the short-*i* words.

in in in in

bib bib bib bib

lick lick lick lick

six six six six

25

Name: _____

PHONICS i
Color
4

Find the short-*i* words. Color them pink.

dig   fish   hen

pig

bug   chick   dog   pin

six   rug   wig   bed

How many blocks have short-*i* words? Circle the number.

1 2 3 4 5 6 ⑦ 8 9 10

26

Name: _____

PHONICS i
Graph
5

Count and graph the short-*i* words.

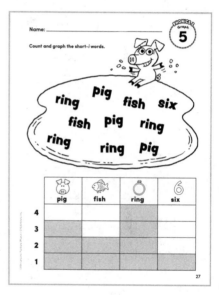

ring pig fish six
fish pig ring
ring ring Pig

	pig	fish	ring	six
4				
3				
2				
1				

27

Name: _____

PHONICS i
Match & Find
6

Draw lines to match the pig with the short-*i* words.

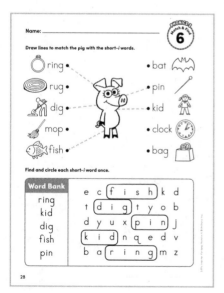

ring •   • bat
rug •   • pin
dig •   • kid
mop •   • clock
fish •   • bag

Find and circle each short-*i* word once.

Word Bank	e c f i s h k d
ring	t d i g t y o b
kid	d y u x p i n j
dig	k i d n q e d v
fish	b a r i n g m z
pin	

28

Name: _____

PHONICS i
Unscramble
7

Unscramble each short-*i* word.

| Word Bank | pig kid wig pin |
| | ring six fish bib |

gip pig   shif fish   wgi wig

nirg ring   ixs six

ibb bib

idk kid   pni pin

29

Name: _____

PHONICS i
Review
8

OINK!

Fill in each short-*i* word once to complete the story. Then read it aloud.

| Word Bank | pig in fish Splish kid wig |

The Pig in a Wig

"Oink!" said the **pig**

She was **in** a boat

with a nice **kid**

Splish, splash!

A **fish** jumped up!

The fish has a big **wig**, too!

GOOD JOB!

30

PACKET 4

PHONICS

short o

PHONICS
short o

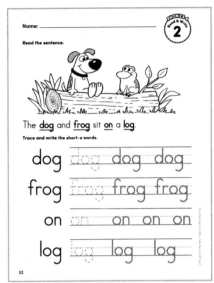

🐕	dog	dog
🦊	fox	fox
🧹	rock	rock
🧹	mop	mop

Trace each word above. Color in each box when you complete the activity.

① Introduction	② Read & Write	③ Read & Write	④ Color
⑤ Graph	⑥ Match & Find	⑦ Unscramble	⑧ Review

31

Name: _____ ②

Read the sentence.

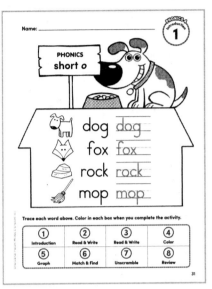

The **dog** and **frog** sit **on** a **log**.

Trace and write the short-o words.

dog   dog   dog dog

frog   frog   frog frog

on   on   on   on

log   log   log log

32

Name: _____ ③

Read the sentence.

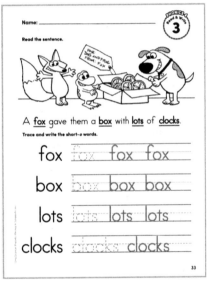

A **fox** gave them a **box** with **lots** of **clocks**.

Trace and write the short-o words.

fox   fox   fox

box   box   box

lots   lots lots

clocks clocks clocks

33

Name: _____ ④

Find the short-o words. Color them 🖍 green.

sock		fish
frog		dog
cat	log	doll	tub
bed	mop	egg	fox

How many blocks have short-o words? Circle the number.

1 2 3 4 5 6 ⑦ 8 9 10

34

Name: _____ ⑤

Count and graph the short-o words.

dog   fox   dog
              rock
fox   dog
   rock   dog
fox   stop

	🐕 dog	🦊 fox	rock	🛑 stop
4				
3				
2				
1				

35

Name: _____ ⑥

Draw lines to match the dog with the short-o words.

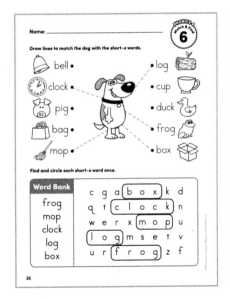

🔔 bell •   • log 🪵
🕐 clock •   • cup ☕
🐷 pig •   • duck 🦆
👜 bag •   • frog 🐸
🧹 mop •   • box 📦

Find and circle each short-o word once.

Word Bank	c g a b o x k d
frog	q t c l o c k n
mop	w e r x m o p u
clock	l o g m s e t v
log	u r f r o g z f
box	

36

Name: _____ ⑦

Unscramble each short-o word.

Word Bank	fox frog ox doll
	mop rock pot sock

🧦 kcos — sock
fxo — fox
cokr — rock
xo — ox
pmo — mop
llod — doll
opt — pot
grof — frog

37

Name: _____ ⑧

Fill in each short-o word once to complete the story. Then read it aloud.

Word Bank	lots tock doll dog sock of

The Box of Clocks

Fox gave __dog__ and frog a box.

The box had __lots__ of clocks!

Some __of__ the clocks were silly.

One clock looked like a pretty __doll__!

One clock looked like a stinky __sock__!

Tick, __tock__!

38

PACKET 5

PHONICS

short *u*

Name: _____

PHONICS
short u

Hi!

duck duck
bus   bus
gum   gum
sun   sun

Trace each word above. Color in each box when you complete the activity.

① Introduction ② Read & Write ③ Read & Write ④ Color
⑤ Graph ⑥ Match & Find ⑦ Unscramble ⑧ Review

39

Name: _____ ②

Read the sentence.

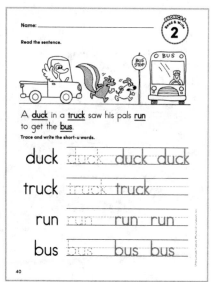

A <u>duck</u> in a <u>truck</u> saw his pals <u>run</u> to get the <u>bus</u>.

Trace and write the short-u words.

duck   duck   duck duck
truck truck truck
run   run   run run
bus   bus   bus bus

40

Name: _____ ③

Read the sentence.

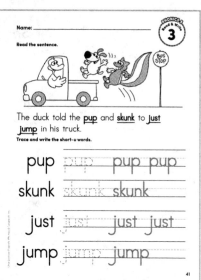

The duck told the <u>pup</u> and <u>skunk</u> to <u>just</u> <u>jump</u> in his truck.

Trace and write the short-u words.

pup   pup   pup pup
skunk skunk skunk
just   just   just just
jump   jump   jump

41

Name: _____ ④

Find the short-u words. Color them 🖍 orange

duck | bug
jug | bag
rock | bus | web | mug
rug | pig | skunk | pup

How many blocks have short-u words? Circle the number.

1 2 3 4 5 6 7 ⑧ 9 10

42

Name: _____ ⑤

Count and graph the short-u words.

sun   bus   duck
duck   gum
    sun
sun   sun   duck
   sun   gum

	🦆 duck	☀ sun	🚌 bus	gum
4				
3				
2				
1				

43

Name: _____ ⑥

Draw lines to match the duck with the short-u words.

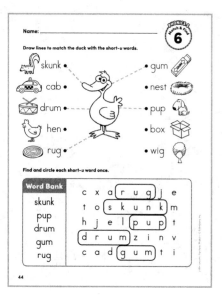

skunk •   • gum
cab •   • nest
drum •   • pup
hen •   • box
rug •   • wig

Find and circle each short-u word once.

Word Bank	
skunk	c x a **r u g** j e
pup	t o **s k u n k** m
drum	h j e l **p u p** t
gum	**d r u m** z i n v
rug	c a d **g u m** t i

44

Name: _____ ⑦

Unscramble each short-u word.

| Word | duck | jug | bug | pup |
| Bank | drum | bus | cup | truck |

gub
bug

uckd
duck

ujg
jug

usb
bus

rumd
drum

puc
cup

upp
pup

kcutr
truck

45

Name: _____ ⑧

Fill in each short-u word once to complete the story. Then read it aloud.

| Word Bank | up | fun | duck | cups | yum | sun |

Up the Hill

The __duck__, pup, and skunk
went __up__ a big hill.
Then they sat in the warm __sun__
and drank __cups__ of tea.
Yum, __yum__!
It was so __fun__!

GOOD JOB!

46

Little Learner Packets: Phonics © Scholastic Inc.

91

PACKET
6
PHONICS
long *a*

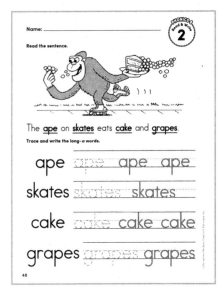

PHONICS long *a*

Hi!

ape — ape
grapes — grapes
rain — rain
train — train

Trace each word above. Color in each box when you complete the activity.

| 1 Introduction | 2 Read & Write | 3 Read & Write | 4 Color |
| 5 Graph | 6 Match & Find | 7 Unscramble | 8 Review |

47

Read the sentence.

The **ape** on **skates** eats **cake** and **grapes**.

Trace and write the long-a words.

ape — ape   ape ape
skates — skates   skates
cake — cake   cake cake
grapes — grapes   grapes

48

Read the sentence.

The ape plays with his **train**, **snail**, and **pail** in the **rain**.

Trace and write the long-a words.

train — train   train train
snail — snail   snail snail
pail — pail   pail pail
rain — rain   rain rain

49

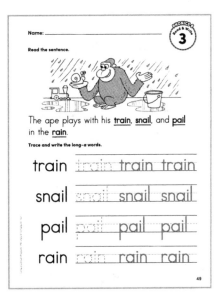

Find the long-a words. Color them **red**.

ape   pail   rain   cave   cake   tail   bee   fox   truck   ring   grapes   pig

How many blocks have long-a words? Circle the number.

1 2 3 4 5 6 (7) 8 9 10

50

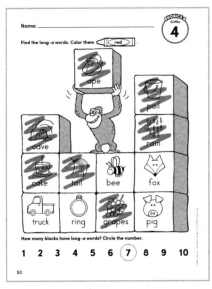

Count and graph the long-a words.

plane   paint   ape   train   plane   paint   plane   paint   train   paint

	ape	plane	train	paint
4				
3				
2				
1				

51

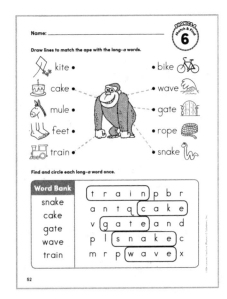

Draw lines to match the ape with the long-a words.

kite •   • bike
cake •   • wave
mule •   • gate
feet •   • rope
train •   • snake

Find and circle each long-a word once.

Word Bank
snake
cake
gate
wave
train

t r a i n p b r
a n t c a k e e
v g a t e a n d
p l s n a k e c
m r p w a v e x

52

Unscramble each long-a word.

Word Bank   pail snake wave cake
rain snail ape nail

pae — ape
ekac — cake
vwae — wave
anir — rain
lasin — snail
naske — snake
liap — pail
ilan — nail

53

I ♥ it!

Ape

Fill in each long-a word once to complete the story. Then read it aloud.

Word Bank   ape whale gave paint made snail

Ape's Painting

The **ape** is an artist.
He loves to **paint**
He **made** a picture
of a **whale** in the rain.
He **gave** it to the snail.
"I love it!" said the **snail**

GOOD JOB!

54

Little Learner Packets: Phonics © Scholastic Inc.

PACKET 7

PHONICS

long e

PHONICS
long e

Hi!

	seal	_seal_
	leaf	_leaf_
	bee	_bee_
	tree	_tree_

Trace each word above. Color in each box when you complete the activity.

1 Introduction	2 Read & Write	3 Read & Write	4 Color
5 Graph	6 Match & Find	7 Unscramble	8 Review

55

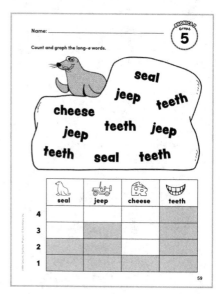

Name: _____ PHONICS 7 Read & Write 2

Read the sentence.

The <u>seal</u> likes to <u>eat</u> ice <u>cream</u> on the <u>beach</u>.

Trace and write the long-e words.

seal _seal_ _seal_ _seal_

eat _eat_ _eat_ _eat_

cream _cream_ _cream_

beach _beach_ _beach_

56

Name: _____ PHONICS 7 Read & Write 3

Read the sentence.

The seal goes to <u>sleep</u> and dreams about <u>three bees</u> and <u>cheese</u>.

Trace and write the long-e words.

sleep _sleep_ _sleep_

three _three_ _three_

bees _bees_ _bees_

cheese _cheese_ _cheese_

57

Name: _____ PHONICS 7 Color 4

Find the long-e words. Color them purple.

seal | tree
beach | mice
queen | skate | feet | leaf
bee | boat | jeans | cube

How many blocks have long-e words? Circle the number.

1 2 3 4 5 6 7 **8** 9 10

58

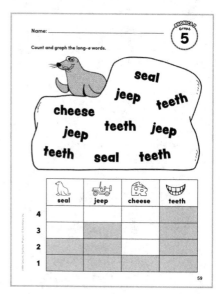

Name: _____ PHONICS 7 Graph 5

Count and graph the long-e words.

seal
jeep teeth
cheese teeth jeep
jeep teeth
teeth seal teeth

seal	jeep	cheese	teeth
4			
3			
2			
1			

59

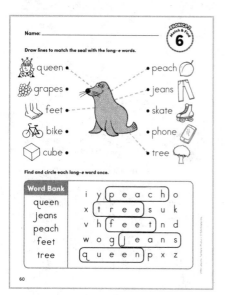

Name: _____ PHONICS 7 Match & Find 6

Draw lines to match the seal with the long-e words.

queen •   • peach
grapes •   • jeans
feet •   • skate
bike •   • phone
cube •   • tree

Find and circle each long-e word once.

Word Bank								
queen	i	y	p	e	a	c	h	o
jeans	x	t	r	e	e	s	u	k
peach	v	h	f	e	e	t	n	d
feet	w	o	g	j	e	a	n	s
tree	q	u	e	e	n	p	x	z

60

Name: _____ PHONICS 7 Unscramble 7

Unscramble each long-e word.

Word Bank	bee	jeep	leaf	feet
	cheese	seal	wheel	sheep

lase _seal_
efet _feet_
fael _leaf_
eechs _cheese_
ebe _bee_
eehwl _wheel_
epje _jeep_
heeps _sheep_

61

Name: _____ PHONICS 7 Review 8

BEEP! BEEP!

Fill in each long-e word once to complete the story. Then read it aloud.

Word Bank	beach	queen	jeep
	sea	beep	sheep

Seal at the Beach

Seal is at a sandy _beach_

He sees a _sheep_

standing in the _sea_

He sees a queen driving

in a _jeep_

The _queen_ toots her horn.

Beep, _beep_ !

GOOD JOB!

62

PACKET
8

PHONICS

long i

Name: _____

PHONICS
long *i* Hi!

mice — mice
kite — kite
ice — ice
five — five

Trace each word above. Color in each box when you complete the activity.

| 1 Introduction | 2 Read & Write | 3 Read & Write | 4 Color |
| 5 Graph | 6 Match & Find | 7 Unscramble | 8 Review |

63

Name: _____

Read the sentence.

The **mice ride** a **bike** as the sun **shines**.

Trace and write the long-*i* words.

mice — mice mice mice
ride — ride ride ride
bike — bike bike bike
shines — shines shines

64

Name: _____

Read the sentence.

The **nice** mice fly **five kites** near a **slide**.

Trace and write the long-*i* words.

nice — nice nice nice
five — five five five
kites — kites kites kites
slide — slide slide slide

65

Name: _____

Find the long-*i* words. Color them 🖍 brown.

mice		seal
slice		fire
ape	bike	mule	dime
five	tree	kite	rope

How many blocks have long-*i* words? Circle the number.

1 2 3 4 5 6 (7) 8 9 10

66

Name: _____

Count and graph the long-*i* words.

nine mice mice
kite nine nine dime
nine mice dime

	mice	kite	nine	dime
4				
3				
2				
1				

67

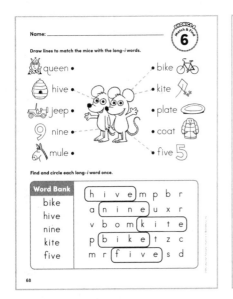

Name: _____

Draw lines to match the mice with the long-*i* words.

queen •   • bike 🚲
hive •   • kite
jeep •   • plate
nine •   • coat
mule •   • five 5

Find and circle each long-*i* word once.

Word Bank
bike
hive
nine
kite
five

h	i	v	e	m	p	b	r
a	n	i	n	e	u	x	r
v	b	o	m	k	i	t	e
p	b	i	k	e	t	z	c
m	r	f	i	v	e	s	d

68

Name: _____

Unscramble each long-*i* word.

Word Bank

| mice | rice | tire | kite |
| ice | fire | nine | hive |

cime — mice
evih — hive
cie — ice
riet — tire
erif — fire
teki — kite
nnei — nine
ceir — rice

69

Name: _____

Fill in each long-*i* word once to complete the story. Then read it aloud.

Word Bank like dive slide cried mice nice

The Nice Pool Party GOOD JOB!

"What a **nice** day for
a pool party!" said the **mice**.
One mouse did a fine **dive**.
One mouse slid down a **slide**.
"We really **like** playing
in the water!" they **cried**.

70

94

Little Learner Packets: Phonics © Scholastic Inc.

PACKET 9

PHONICS

long o

Name: _____

PHONICS
long o

Hi!

goat goat
boat boat
nose nose
rope rope

Trace each word above. Color in each box when you complete the activity.

| ① Introduction | ② Read & Write | ③ Read & Write | ④ Color |
| ⑤ Graph | ⑥ Match & Find | ⑦ Unscramble | ⑧ Review |

71

Name: _____

Read the sentence.

The **goat** wears a **coat** when he **floats** in a **boat**.

Trace and write the long-o words.

goat goat goat goat
coat coat coat coat
floats floats floats
boat boat boat boat

72

Name: _____

Read the sentence.

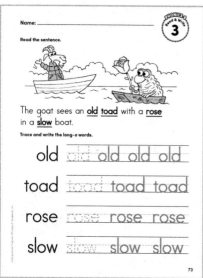

The goat sees an **old toad** with a **rose** in a **slow** boat.

Trace and write the long-o words.

old old old old old
toad toad toad toad
rose rose rose rose
slow slow slow slow

73

Name: _____

Find the long-o words. Color them grey.

How many blocks have long-o words? Circle the number.

1 2 3 4 5 6 7 ⑧ 9 10

74

Name: _____

Count and graph the long-o words.

goat rose
soap soap rose
smoke soap
goat goat soap

	goat	soap	rose	smoke
4		▓		
3	▓	▓		
2	▓	▓	▓	
1	▓	▓	▓	▓

75

Name: _____

Draw lines to match the goat with the long-o words.

soap •   • cube
bike •   • boat
phone •   • nose
jeep •   • rain
rope •   • snail

Find and circle each long-o word once.

Word Bank
boat
soap
phone
nose
rope

| r o p e k e q z |
| a b h s o a p w |
| g p h o n e i d |
| n o s e m y u t |
| t g a b o a t c |

76

Name: _____

7

Unscramble each long-o word.

Word Bank
| nose | soap | rope | road |
| boat | goat | phone | hole |

taog → goat
posa → soap
atob → boat
poer → rope
adro → road
seno → nose
leho → hole
enoph → phone

77

Name: _____

THE FROG WAS SO HOPPY!

HA! HA! HA!

Fill in each long-o word once to complete the story. Then read it aloud.

Word Bank phone goat joke toad so boat

The Goat in a Boat

The goat in a **boat**
uses his cell **phone**
to call the old **toad**
Then the **goat**
tells the old toad a **joke**
The joke is **so** funny!

GOOD JOB!

78

PACKET 10

PHONICS

long *u*

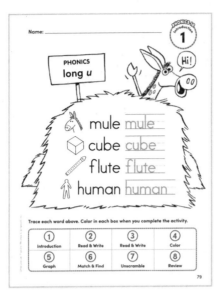

PHONICS 10
Introduction
1

PHONICS
long *u*

Hi!

mule mule
cube cube
flute flute
human human

Trace each word above. Color in each box when you complete the activity.

| ① Introduction | ② Read & Write | ③ Read & Write | ④ Color |
| ⑤ Graph | ⑥ Match & Find | ⑦ Unscramble | ⑧ Review |

79

PHONICS 10
Read & Write
2

Read the sentence.

The <u>cute mule</u> stood on a <u>huge cube</u>.

Trace and write the long-u words.

cute   cute cute cute
mule   mule mule mule
huge   huge huge huge
cube   cube cube cube

80

PHONICS 10
Read & Write
3

Read the sentence.

The mule <u>used</u> a <u>flute</u> to play <u>music</u> for a <u>unicorn</u>.

Trace and write the long-u words.

used   used used used
flute   flute flute flute
music   music music
unicorn unicorn unicorn

81

PHONICS 10
Color
4

Find the long-u words. Color them [blue].

mule
dune   flute   cube
bee   music   feet   boat
cave   tube   ape   unicorn

How many blocks have long-u words? Circle the number.

1 2 3 4 5 6 ⑦ 8 9 10

82

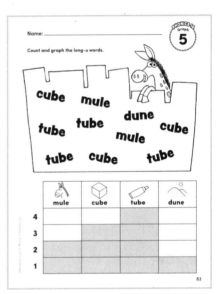

PHONICS 10
Graph
5

Count and graph the long-u words.

cube   mule
dune
tube   tube   cube
mule
tube   cube   tube

	mule	cube	tube	dune
4				
3				
2				
1				

83

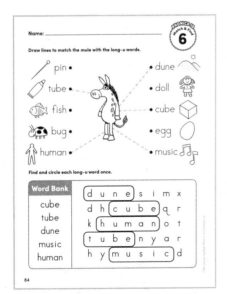

PHONICS 10
Match & Find
6

Draw lines to match the mule with the long-u words.

pin •   • dune
tube •   • doll
fish •   • cube
bug •   • egg
human •   • music

Find and circle each long-u word once.

Word Bank
cube
tube
dune
music
human

d u n e s i m x
d h c u b e q r
k h u m a n o t
t u b e n y a r
h y m u s i c d

84

PHONICS 10
Unscramble
7

Unscramble each long-u word.

Word Bank	mule bugle dune cube
	flute music tube unicorn

elum   beut   ebcu
mule   tube   cube

etulf   simcu
nedu   flute   music
dune

corninu glueb
unicorn bugle

85

PHONICS 10
Review
8

Fill in each long-u word once to complete the story. Then read it aloud.

| Word Bank | bugle mule huge flute unicorn cube |

The Mule and the Unicorn

The mule has spots!
The unicorn has stars!
They sit on a cube
It is so huge
The mule plays a flute
The unicorn plays a bugle
They make beautiful music!

GOOD JOB!

86
